DEVOTIONS
galore!

warm-ups, wrap-ups, and prayers
for women's groups

Group

Group resources actually work!

This Group resource incorporates our R.E.A.L. approach to ministry. It reinforces a growing friendship with Jesus, encourages long-term learning, and results in life transformation, because it's

Relational
Learner-to-learner interaction enhances learning and builds Christian friendships.

Experiential
What learners experience through discussion and action sticks with them up to 9 times longer than what they simply hear or read.

Applicable
The aim of Christian education is to equip learners to be both hearers and doers of God's Word.

Learner-based
Learners understand and retain more when the learning process takes into consideration how they learn best.

Devotions Galore
Warm-Ups, Wrap-Ups, and Prayers for Women's Groups
Copyright © 2008 Group Publishing, Inc.

Visit our website: **www.group.com/women**

Credits
Our Delightfully Devoted Contributors: Jody Brolsma, Gina Leuthauser, Chey Macalik, Jennifer Moe, Lori Poppinga, Margot Starbuck, Roxanne Wieman

Executive Developer: Amy Nappa

Chief Creative Officer: Joani Schultz

Copy Editor: Kate Nickel

Cover Designer: Samantha Wranosky

Art Director: Andrea Filer

Book Designer and Print Production Artist: Greg Longbons, Kadence Ainsworth

Production Manager: DeAnne Lear

Photography: Rodney Stewart

Unless otherwise indicated, all Scripture quotations are taken from the *Holy Bible,* New Living Translation, copyright © 1996, 2004. Used by permission of Tyndale House Publishers, Inc., Carol Stream, Illinois 60188. All rights reserved.

Library of Congress Cataloging-in-Publication Data
Devotions galore : warm-ups, wrap-ups, and prayers for women's group /
[contributors, Jody Brolsma ... et al.].
    p. cm.
  Includes index.
  ISBN 978-0-7644-3695-6 (pbk. : alk. paper)
  1. Church work with women. 2. Women--Prayers and devotions. I.
Brolsma, Jody. II. Group Publishing.
  BV4445.D48 2008
  242'.643--dc22
                                    2008001710
ISBN 978-0-7644-3695-6
10 9 8 7 6 5 4 3 2   17 16 15 14 13 12 11 10
Printed in the United States of America.

Introduction 5

Warm~Ups

Wrap~Ups

Contents

Prayers

Scripture Index

Contents

Introduction

Hello! If you're holding this book in your hands, you're probably involved in a women's group of some kind. Perhaps you're a Bible study leader. Or maybe you're speaking at an upcoming retreat. You might have been asked to provide a devotion to begin or end a baby or bridal shower, or you may be the person who leads a weekly prayer gathering. Or maybe you just love women and want to find creative ways to draw them closer to Jesus. Well, this is the book for you!

On the following pages you'll find thirty different ways to *start* a meeting, Bible study, or other gathering that will immediately engage women and open their minds and hearts to your topic. These are the warm-ups.

You'll also find thirty different ways to *end* a meeting, bringing your time of discussion or study to a close in a meaningful way that will keep the topic rumbling around in their minds and encourage application for days and weeks beyond your gathering. These are the wrap-ups.

You'll also find thirty unique *prayer* activities that will engage women's hearts as they express their thoughts and emotions to God in creative ways. Some are reflective, some are active, and all of them are God-focused. These are the prayers.

How to Use Devotions Galore

If you glance at the Table of Contents for this book, you'll notice that there are 30 topics covered. There are warm-ups, wrap-ups, and prayers for these 30 topics, so you have 90 ideas to choose from. This means you can...

- Use just one idea for your gathering. Choose just the warm-up, just the wrap-up, or just the prayer that works best for you.

- Pair two ideas that follow the same topic. Pair a warm-up with a wrap-up, or pair a warm-up with a prayer, or a wrap-up with a prayer...you get the idea!

- Use all three ideas for one topic to *really* make your life easy!

We've also provided a handy *Scripture Index* at the end of the book. Any devotion that uses a specific Bible passage or that has been tailored to fit with a group of verses—we've put those all in one handy list so you can search for a verse you're discussing and find a fresh idea to use with it!

Handy Tips

Lead like a pro with these helpful hints:

- Any time women are talking in pairs or small groups, play music softly in the background. This creates a nice atmosphere in your room and helps women feel less self-conscience about sharing aloud. You'll also want to play reflective music during many of the prayer activities—it really helps set the mood.

- If you are doing a devotion that lists several questions for women to discuss in pairs or small groups, write these on a white board, chalk board, newsprint, or put them on a media slide so women can refer to them during the allotted discussion time. This lets them move through the discussion at their own pace, without you interrupting them to share the next question.

- Discussions always go more smoothly if women are in smaller groups. Three to five women is generally ideal as it gives time for each person to share, and doesn't put a lot of pressure on one person to do all the talking.

Warm~Ups

Balance

Sometimes having too heavy of a burden is what throws us off balance in life. Open with this activity that will help women *experience* what it feels like to have their burdens lifted.

Prep and Supplies

NO PREP

Tip

This is a good intro to a session on Matthew 11:28-30.

The Warm-Up

Have women get into groups of three and stand next to one another. Ask the two women on the outside of the trio to hold down the middle woman's arms while she tries as hard as she can to raise them. Use a clock or stopwatch, and have women let go of their partner's arms after 30 seconds. Switch roles so that each woman gets to be in the middle.

Ahh, didn't it feel good to have your burdens lifted?

Have groups discuss:

- *Quick, name all of the words that come to mind that describe how it felt to have your arms held down.*

- *How about when your arms were released?*

- *When have you felt like this after having a burden in your life lifted?*

- *How does having a heavy burden throw you off balance in life?*

Continue with your session.

Beauty

This skit is a funny reminder of how far we go to look "beautiful."

Prep and Supplies

- cosmetic bag of supplies as explained

You'll need two women to participate in a short sketch with you. Choose women ahead of time who are willing to ham it up and get a little messy, and meet with them before your session to go over the basics of the skit. It's an improvisation skit, so there is no script to follow—you'll all just go with the flow (and the laughter) and have fun.

This skit requires two people to create one performer as shown. This works best if the taller person is in the front. Using this method, the woman in front speaks but does not use her hands, while the woman in back is silent but does all the hand motions and actions. We'll refer to them as the Speaker and the Hands.

Gather a number of cosmetics in an overnight case. When you are ready to do the skit, introduce only the Speaker (or perhaps combine their names into one name so that Jennifer and Kimberly become "Jennikim"). You'll then interview the Speaker. Open the bag, pull out an item, and ask the Speaker how she'll use this as you give the item to the Hands. The Hands will demonstrate how to use the item, while the Speaker has no choice but to go along. This is funniest if you include items such as bright lipstick and eye shadow, an unplugged curling iron, a hair brush, and perhaps even a bit of shaving cream with a disposable razor (with the cap covering the blade!).

You'll use this skit to demonstrate that we, as women, often cover our flaws and hide behind our beauty products. So be sure your dramatic assistants ham it up and go wild with the primping as they interact with you.

The Warm-Up

Have the women you've worked with ahead of time come up to be "interviewed" by you. Explain that this guest is a beauty expert, and she's going to be sharing her secret tips with everyone.

You'll pull various items from the case, ask the Speaker how (in her expert opinion) they should be used, and have the Hands demonstrate. Because the Hands can't see very well, the Speaker will end up with eye makeup on her cheeks or forehead, lipstick on her nose, and so on.

When several items have been demonstrated and your skit team is thoroughly "made up," thank your assistants for helping, and have everyone give them a round of applause.

Say: *I'm sure many of you can relate to this skit. We want to look great, so we go through all kinds of trouble to cover up. But God wants us to come to him just as we are, blemishes and all!*

Continue with your session.

Contentment

It's amazing how little things can bring us great comfort. This warm-up challenges women to identify what comforts them.

Prep and Supplies

NO PREP

The Warm-Up

Have women form groups of four or five. Explain that each woman needs to find one item she has with her (that she's wearing, is in a pocket, or in her purse) that somehow represents comfort to her. Don't give too many examples—you want women to come up with their own ideas for this one.

Allow about one minute for women to find an item, and then have them go around their groups and tell about their item and how it represents comfort. A woman might show her cell phone and tell that she feels comforted by being in contact with her family. Another might have lip balm and explain that this represents small physical things that comfort her. Clothing, money, business cards…all of these and more are items women will have on them that could represent comfort.

Allow about five minutes for sharing, and then ask:

- *What was the funniest or most unusual thing someone in your group shared?*

- *How is it that we can find contentment in such small items…but usually long for much bigger items to bring us contentment?*

Continue with your session.

Forgiveness

This warm-up gets women thinking about the completeness of God's forgiveness.

Prep and Supplies

- white butcher paper
- colored and regular pencils
- erasers

Cover each table with white paper. At each table place several regular and colored pencils—at least one pencil per woman. Make sure there's also at least one large pencil eraser at each table.

Tip

If you don't have large sheets of paper to cover tables, you can just provide big pieces of white paper.

This session uses Isaiah 1:18 as a starting point.

The Warm-Up

Invite women to take a few moments to draw doodles on the paper as they visit with each other. Encourage them to cover as much of the paper as possible, making their table colorful and decorative.

After about five minutes, ask the women to pass around the eraser and erase the doodles they've made. Then ask:

- *Was anyone able to erase their drawings so completely that you can't see the mark any more and the paper looks completely clean?*

Say: *The Bible tells us that sin is like these doodles. All of us sin. There's not one of us who hasn't lied, cheated, or taken something, even a little something, that wasn't ours to take. Many people spend their lives feeling terrible guilt for the wrong things they've done. Other religions teach that by doing good things or by living a spiritual life that you can make up for the wrong that you've done. But that's not what the Bible teaches. The Bible says that there's nothing we can do to make up for our sins. It's like trying to erase pencil marks from this paper. There's no way we can make the paper look brand new again. Listen to these words from the Bible. "Come now, let's settle this," says the Lord. "Though your sins are like scarlet, I will make them as white as snow. Though they are red like crimson, I will make them as white as wool" (Isaiah 1:18).*

Continue with your session.

Friendship

This warm-up will help women discover how friends build us up and stick with us.

Prep and Supplies

- interlocking blocks in a variety of shapes and sizes

Tip

Check out the nursery or children's ministry area of your church to see if you can borrow a box of interlocking blocks.

The Warm-Up

Have women form groups of three and give each person a handful of interlocking blocks. Ask each woman to choose one block and place that in her hand.

Say: *This block will represent you.*

Then direct women to go around their trios and take turns adding new blocks to their own. Each time a woman adds a block, she should say the name of a special friend and tell how that person "stuck" with her. For example, "Holly, who stuck with me during sophomore P.E." or "Cathy, who stuck with me during a hard time at work."

After about five minutes, have women display their creations to show how our friends build us up and stick with us. Have trios discuss:

- *How do friends make us stronger?*

- *What makes some friendships really "stick" like these blocks stick together?*

Continue with your session.

Gentleness

This activity helps women consider how it feels to be around someone who has a gentle spirit.

Prep and Supplies

- several itchy wool clothing items such as a sweater, cap, gloves, or scarf

- several soft fabric clothing items such as those made of silk, satin, or fleece

Tip

This session uses Colossians 3:12.

The Warm-Up

Have women form groups of up to five. Give each group one of the itchy items and one of the soft items—but don't describe them for the women. Just say something like "Here are a few items you're going to be using as we get started."

When each group has their items, say:

Pass these clothing items around, and say the first word that comes to mind as you feel the fabric.

After a few minutes, have groups call out some of the words they used. You're sure to hear a few *soft, cozy, gentle* words mixed in with *scratchy, irritating,* and *harsh.*

Have groups discuss:

- *Which garment would you rather wear all day long? Why?*

- *If these fabrics represented a person, which would you rather be around all day long? Explain.*

- *Colossians 3:12 says, "Since God chose you to be the holy people he loves, you must clothe yourselves with tenderhearted mercy, kindness, humility, gentleness, and patience." How do you think we can clothe ourselves in gentleness?*

Allow time between each question for groups to talk. After the last question, have a few groups report their thoughts to the larger group.

Continue with your session.

God's Plan/God's Will

It's important to do things in the right order. Use this warm-up to make the point that in seeking God's will for our lives we must first start with *him*. When we put *him* first, knowing his will for us becomes much clearer.

The Warm-Up

Distribute the different pages with baking instructions to the women, giving one to each woman. If your group is large, form pairs or groups of three and give one to every small group.

Explain that you need a bit of help with your cookie recipe and would like for them to try to put it back into the correct order. Provide tape and a place on a wall to hang the recipe steps in order. Give women a few minutes to work together to see if they can get the recipe back in the right order. When they're finished, read the original recipe aloud and check their work. In smaller groups, discuss these questions, allowing groups to share a few answers with the larger group before sharing the next question:

- *Why is it important to follow the step-by-step instructions of a recipe?*

- *How is following a recipe in the right order like or unlike following God's will?*

- *What do you think God wants you to do first in your life in order to accomplish his will for you?*

Continue with your session.

Prep and Supplies

- tape

- paper

Write out a basic cookie recipe of your choice with each step written on separate sheets of paper in large writing. For example, one sheet of paper will say, "Beat eggs", another will say, "Preheat oven to 350 degrees" and so on. Have the original recipe with you to refer to later.

Tip

Matthew 10:39 is a great verse to use as you discuss seeking God's will. For a special treat, bake the cookies in your recipe ahead of time and have them ready to share at the end of this warm-up.

Goodness

God's goodness is all around us. This warm-up will be a reminder of the evidence of God's goodness in our own lives.

Prep and Supplies

- Bibles or copies of Acts 14:17
- paper
- pens or pencils
- watch

Tip

This warm-up uses Acts 14:17.

The Warm-Up

Have the women form groups of three or four. Be sure that each group has either a Bible or a copy of Acts 14:17 ("…but he never left them without evidence of himself and his goodness. For instance, he sends you rain and good crops and gives you food and joyful hearts.") and paper and pen or pencil.

Say: *You've got three minutes to read Acts 14:17 and list as many evidences of God's goodness as you can. To make it a little more challenging, I'd like you to list only evidences that those of you in your group have experienced. Everyone ready? Begin!*

After three minutes, have each group share two or three of the items from their lists. Be sure each group tells how many items they were able to list—just as a way of everyone seeing that we can come up with fairly decent lists when we stop to think about it!

Continue with your session.

Grace

This warm-up reminds women that it's God's grace that draws us to him, and the relationship we receive by grace is a warm and wonderful gift.

Prep and Supplies

- several large bowls of ice
- several blow dryers or electric blankets
- watch with a second hand

Place the bowls of ice on tables around your room. Plug in the electric blankets and turn them on ahead of time so they'll be warm. Leave them on a low setting and place them around the room as well.

Tip

If you don't have access to electric blankets, you can use blow dryers instead. Be sure you have a volunteer to hold each blow dryer and blow it on the hands of women at the appropriate time.

The Warm-Up

Have women stand around the bowls of ice.

Say: *When I give the signal, I'd like you all to put your hands into the bowls of ice and see if you can keep them there for 30 seconds. While your hands are in the bowl, quickly say words that compare this icy experience to sin. How is sin like this icy experience? Ready? Begin!*

After 30 seconds, have women immediately move over to the warm blankets and place their hands on or under them.

As they stand there warming their freezing hands, have them discuss how God's grace is like the warmth of the blanket.

After a few minutes of warming and sharing, have the group return to their seats. Let a few women share their comparisons of the icy experience to sin (perhaps they'll say sin is cold, hard, you want to get out of it). Then allow a few women to share their comparisons of the warm blanket to God's grace (they might say it's a relief, soothing, healing, soft).

Say: *Grace is a gift God gives us—we don't deserve it and it's not "owed" to us. There are many people who are longing to experience the warmth of God's grace. Let's spend a little more time learning about this amazing gift God has given us.*

Continue with your session.

Hope

God's Word is teeming with hope for each of us!
This activity helps women search out the hope
we have in Jesus.

The Warm-Up

Have women form groups of three or four. Be sure each
group has a Bible, paper, and pen or pencil.

Say: *Your challenge is to see how many verses you can
find that have the word* hope *(or* hopeful, hoping, *and so
on), and list those. No fair using a concordance or other
index! Assign one woman in each group the task of writing
down the reference and whether the verse is full of hope or
is about being hopeless.*

After about five to 10 minutes, have each group share the
total number of verses found. Let each group share their
favorite verse aloud with the larger group.

Have groups discuss:

- *Did you realize there were so many references to
  hope in the Bible?*

- *What does that say to you personally about God's
  desire for your life?*

Continue with your session.

Prep and Supplies

- Bibles
- paper
- pens or pencils
- watch

Tip

The Bible contains
over 150 verses
on hope, many of
which are found
in Psalms and
Proverbs. If your
group has many
women who are
not very familiar
with the Bible,
have them focus
on these two
books for this
activity.

Integrity

A woman with integrity strives to develop her inner life, not just her outer appearance. This warm-up helps women consider the value of integrity.

Prep and Supplies

- One fake jewelry item per woman. Choose obviously cheap and fake jewelry such as toy children's jewelry or party favors from a discount store.

The Warm-Up

Have women form groups of three or four. Give each woman a piece of the fake jewelry to examine as groups discuss these questions:

- *Describe how your piece of jewelry looks and feels.*

- *Compare the jewelry you've been given to whatever jewelry you or someone else in your group is wearing right now. How are the items alike? How are they different? How can you tell which one is of more value?*

- *Look at the jewelry you were given and the real jewelry worn by women in your group. Which pieces could you use the word "integrity" to describe?*

Move into a discussion of the difference between outward appearance and the integrity that comes from true internal character, and the value God places on that inner integrity.

Continue with your session.

Joy

This warm-up reminds women that joy comes from God, not our circumstances.

Prep and Supplies

- index cards

Prepare one index card per woman by writing one of the following statements on each card. It's OK to repeat cards—just be sure you always have two cards that "match."

- I am getting married.
- I am going through a divorce.
- I have extra time each day to relax.
- I am stressed every last minute of the day.
- I just got a promotion!
- I just lost my job.
- I have many friends.
- I am lonely.
- My child is peaceful and easy-going.
- My toddler is driving me crazy!

The Warm-Up

Distribute one card to each woman. Explain that each card has an opposite card. Have women move around and find a person whose card seems likely to be the opposite of her own.

When each person has found a partner, say: *Imagine for a moment that the words on your card describe your life right now. Take one minute each to describe how you are feeling based on what your card says.*

Tip

Psalm 31:7 and Psalm 59:16 both work nicely with this warm-up.

After two minutes, ask if anyone used the word "joy" to describe her feelings in this conversation. If anyone did, have a few of those women tell which card they have and why this situation might cause joy. Then ask pairs to discuss:

- *Do you think it's possible to find joy in the situation described on your card? Why or why not?*

Use this to lead into a time of exploring how we can find joy in God, no matter what our life circumstances are.

Continue with your session.

Kindness

Kindness is a fruit of the Spirit, and, according to Philemon 1:7, it's refreshing to be shown kindness. Use this warm-up to get women talking about kindness and exploring how it truly does "refresh the heart."

The Warm-Up

Hand out the index cards or sticky notes and ask everyone to write down one way they either showed kindness or received kindness in the past week.

Once everyone has finished writing, ask women to fold up their cards or notes and put them in the basket or hat that you'll pass around the room. Shuffle the notes inside, and then pass the basket or hat around the room and tell everyone to grab one note. (They should be sure they don't get their own note.)

After everyone has a note, have women pair up and discuss the following questions with their partner:

- *How would you define kindness?*
- *How was kindness shown in the note you drew?*
- *How do you think that act of kindness "refreshed" the person who received it?*
- *How have you been refreshed by an act of kindness?*

Continue with your session.

Prep and Supplies

- one index card or sticky note per person
- a basket or hat

Tip

This warm-up works well with Philemon 1:7.

Loneliness

This warm-up experience draws on the feelings associated with loneliness, and reminds women that we all have these feelings—and can turn to God with them.

Prep and Supplies

NO PREP

Tip

This warm-up uses Psalm 102:7.

The Warm-Up

Have women stand facing the walls of the room. If they can literally be almost touching the wall and looking right at it, so they can't see others around them, that's best. Anyone who cannot be close to a wall should at least close her eyes so she cannot see others.

Say: *Quiet your thoughts for a moment, and think back to a time when you felt very lonely. Some of you might have to think back a ways. Some of you might have felt this way in the last 10 minutes. Quietly remember the feelings of loneliness.*

Pause for about 15 seconds.

Say: *Psalm 102: 7 says, "I lie awake, lonely as a solitary bird on the roof."*

As you think on this passage, call out one word or one sentence that describes how loneliness feels. Do this standing where you are.

Allow one or two minutes for women to randomly call out words or thoughts. You may hear words like *alone, sad, peaceful, hurting,* and other similar feelings.

After about two minutes, say: *Turn around and take the hand of one or two women nearby.*

When each woman has done this, say, *Psalm 145:18 says, "The LORD is close to all who call on him, yes, to all who call on him in truth." James 4:8 says, "Come close to God, and God will come close to you." God is closer than the hand of the person next to you.*

Have women return to their seats and continue your session.

Love

Prep and Supplies

NO PREP

Sometimes loving those around us feels ooey-gooey and sappy-sweet. Other times, it's down-right difficult! This activity lets women share about those various relationships.

The Warm-Up

Have women form groups of three or four and introduce themselves to each other.

When groups are ready, say: *We're going to play a game with several rounds. For this round, the person in your group wearing the most blue will answer first. I'll call out a category and the person wearing the most blue will say the name of the first person in that category who comes to mind. Ready? The first category is "neighbor."*

Wait until the person wearing the most blue in each group has called out the name of the first neighbor that comes to mind.

Say: *Now I'd like you to share with your group about this person. Is this person easy to love or hard to love, and why? You have one minute.*

After a minute call out a new category, and be sure to choose a different color of clothing to indicate which person in the group should answer for this round. Categories you might include are:

- parents
- children
- co-workers
- siblings
- girlfriends
- guy friends

After you've played a few rounds and everyone has shared at least once, continue with your session.

Obedience

Our lives are full of many different voices and influences which often make it difficult to listen only to the voice of God and do what *he* says. This warm-up reminds women that obedience to God is vital to living an abundant Christian life.

Prep and Supplies

NO PREP

The Warm-Up

Ask a volunteer to leave the room. Explain to her that when she returns she will be told what to do next.

When the volunteer has left the room, explain to the other women that when she returns they are to begin giving her different directions, all at the same time. For example, one person (or group of women) could tell her to go to her chair, one could tell her to pick up her purse, and at the same time another person could tell her to go to the door, and so on. For extra fun, be sure some of the directions directly contradict others. When everyone is ready, call the volunteer back into the room and let the chaos begin!

After a minute or so of this activity, let the volunteer take her seat. Ask her how she felt during the activity. Talk about how just like in the activity, we can easily become overwhelmed and even confused with all the voices and influences in our lives. We need to learn to "tune out" all these distractions in our lives that keep us from being fully attentive to God's voice and doing what *he* wants us to do.

Continue with your session.

Patience

Patience is a virtue that we all wish we had more of, but that we don't want to, well, wait for! You can use this warm-up to get women discussing patience in their own lives while they experience waiting for something tasty.

Prep and Supplies

- one delicious treat (such as a brownie, cookie, or slice of cheesecake) per person

Be sure the treats are nicely displayed, and that they are on individual plates or napkins so women can take one easily. Do not serve any other snacks ahead of time so women will be nice and hungry!

The Warm-Up

Have women find partners, introduce themselves, and sit together. Give each woman one of your delicious treats. Tell them to hold their treat in front of them, but they are not to eat it just yet.

Say: *While you're holding this treat and imagining how delicious it will taste, talk to your partner about the times in your life when you feel the most impatient.*

After three or four minutes, invite a few women to share their responses with the entire group. At this time you can let women know they don't have to be impatient any more, and they may eat their treat. Or, if you really want to drive home the point, you might consider having them really exercise patience and wait until the end of your gathering to indulge!

Continue with your session.

Peace

Use this warm-up to introduce the idea that we have a measure of control when it comes to embracing the peace God offers to us. It's a gift from God that we often allow to be taken away.

The Warm-Up

Begin your meeting by playing the dissonant song for the group. Make sure it's loud enough to really annoy the women in your meeting. Let it play until women are agitated.

Stop the music, and then ask them to share their emotions and feelings as the music played.

After several women have shared, note that anyone could have stopped the music at any time by simply pushing a button on the CD player. Have women form groups of four. Play the peaceful song and as it plays have women discuss:

- *Why didn't you stop the annoying music?*
- *What are things in your life that rob your peace that you have the power to stop?*
- *Why don't you always stop those peace-robbers?*
- *How can you fight for peace in your life?*
- *What will it take to win the fight?*

Continue with your session.

Prep and Supplies

- CD
- CD player

Find the most grating, annoying, discontent, and dissonant song you can get a hold of. Find a peaceful song to play also. If you have trouble finding a good song to use, ask the youth pastor or someone in the youth group to help you.

Pride

Scripture says that God opposes the proud. When you think of all the pain it causes others and us, it's no wonder that God doesn't have much tolerance for pride. Use this warm-up to help women get in touch with and let go of their own pride.

Prep and Supplies

- 1 helium balloon
- 1 uninflated balloon per woman
- pens
- slips of paper

Tip

This passage uses Jeremiah 9:23-24 and James 4:10.

The Warm-Up

Read Jeremiah 9:23 aloud.

Say: *This passage mentions things we should not be boastful or proud about: wisdom, power, or riches. Think about what you're most likely to be boastful or proud about. It might be your intelligence or your power or your riches, or other things not mentioned here. Write those things on slips of paper. Use one slip for each thing you're likely to be boastful or proud about. You won't have to share these with anyone else.*

When each woman has a few slips of paper completed, have them fold their slips and put them into an uninflated balloon, and then blow up the balloon and tie it. Then tell women they'll need to bat these into the air and keep them aloft for one whole minute. (For a bit of fun play music for a minute to add to the ambiance.)

After a minute, have women find their balloons and sit down again. Ask a few to share how hard or easy it was to keep their balloons in the air. Then say: *It can be tiring trying to lift ourselves up in the eyes of others. Pride can be a lot of work! The Bible told us what we should not be boastful about. Let's hear what we should be boastful about.*

Read Jeremiah 9:23-24 and allow women to reflect on this for a moment. Ask how lifting God up and boasting about him would be easier than lifting ourselves up in the eyes of others.

Read James 4:10, and hold out the helium balloon for all to see. Ask women to discuss with a partner how God lifts us up when we are humble instead of boastful and proud.

Continue with your session.

Purity

Use this warm-up to introduce the idea that there isn't anything we can do to make ourselves pure. Only Jesus can make us pure.

Prep and Supplies

- 1 clear, empty glass
- 1 pitcher of water
- a small container of bleach

The Warm-Up

Show the group the empty glass and the water. Pour the water into the glass and take a sip. Talk about how the water is pure, and you've demonstrated this purity by being willing to drink it.

Then add a large splash of bleach to the water. Ask for volunteers to take a drink of the water now. Ask how you could make the water pure again. Talk about how the only way you could make the water pure again is to start with new water. Note that we can't make ourselves pure. Only Jesus forgiving our sins and making us new can restore our purity.

Continue with your session.

Purpose

Want to get women thinking about their purpose in life? Use this warm-up to get started!

Prep and Supplies

- paper and pencils

The Warm-Up

Have women get into small groups of four or five. Have each group work together to create a list of at least 10 famous women and what they are famous for doing.

After several minutes of brainstorming, have women stop and listen.

Say: *Look at the women on your list. As you read through them again together, I'd like you to do two things. First, see if you can guess what each woman might say was her purpose in life. Second, discuss how you think these women knew what their purpose was.*

After five to 10 minutes of group discussion, have a few of the groups share some of their thoughts with the larger group. Then continue with your session.

Self~Control

Closely related to discipline and restraint, self-control is no one's favorite topic. However, you can use this warm-up to start a discussion on the importance of self-control to help Christians live *in* the world without being *of* the world.

Prep and Supplies

• chairs

Tip

This warm-up works well with Titus 2:11-13.

The Warm-Up

Have everyone stand up and put her hands on the back of a chair or on another stable surface. Now ask women to balance on one foot while still holding on to the back of the chair. Go for about a minute, then challenge women to let go of the chair and balance on one foot without support for another minute. Count down the last ten seconds of the minute as women continue to balance. After the minute is up, have women pair up to discuss these questions:

• *How did this activity require self-control?*

• *When are you most challenged to be self-controlled?*

• *What did you learn from this activity that could help you with self-control?*

• *Do you think self-control is an important Christian attribute? Why or why not?*

Continue with your session.

Service

This warm-up will help women rethink what it means to treat others as they would want to be treated.

Prep and Supplies

- paper and pens

Tip

This warm-up uses Galatians 5:14.

The Warm-Up

Read Galatians 5:14 aloud. Note that this verse often makes us think of how we *shouldn't* treat people; we *shouldn't* be mean to others because we don't want others to be mean to us.

Say: *Let's think about this verse in a positive light. What good thing would you like done for you?*

Have women work in pairs or trios to make lists of things they would enjoy others doing for *them*. It can be simple things such as receiving a "thinking about you" card, getting a phone call in the middle of the day from a friend, or being invited to a movie. After several minutes, invite each pair or small group to share one or two items from their list with the entire group.

Encourage each woman to pick one thing from the list to put into action. Have them think of a person they could do one of these things for, and do it. Talk about how good it feels to *really love* your neighbor as yourself!

Continue with your session.

Sharing Your Faith

This skit brings a Bible story about a woman sharing her faith to life in a humorous way.

Prep and Supplies

You'll need a man's hat; a bottle of water; a large purse or tote bag that has a funny hat, a pair of sunglasses, and a cell phone inside; and a microphone.

This is an "instant" skit—your volunteers will act based on what you read. When you're ready to begin, select two volunteers from your group. Give one a man's hat and a bottle of water. She will be Jesus and should stand to the side of the stage area. Give the other woman a large purse or tote bag that has a funny hat, a pair of sunglasses, and a cell phone inside. Add to the humor by including other items in the purse that she'll have to dig through to find the items she needs. Set a microphone to the side that this woman can use when the script directs her to do so.

The Warm-Up

Explain that neither actress has ever seen this script. **Say:** *I'll read the story, and they'll act it out. If a character says something, I'll say it first, and they'll repeat it after me.*

Tip

This warm-up uses the account of Jesus talking to the woman at the well from John 4.

Read the "Jesus on Aisle Three" script, encouraging your actresses to ham it up as they participate. When the skit is over, have everyone give the actresses a huge round of applause.

Jesus on Aisle Three

There was a woman from Samaria who needed to go to the store for water. She was thirsty...parched...sticking her tongue out and grasping at her throat, she was so in need of water. But she had a reputation around town and didn't want to be seen. So she covered her head with a hat...put on some dark glasses...and went to the store acting more like a spy than a thirsty woman.

She dodged behind a canned-food display when she saw the town gossip...she crawled on her hands and knees under a pyramid of produce when she saw another woman...she *had* to get to the bottled water aisle! Finally, she rounded the corner sharply...sharply!...and bumped into a man.

After brushing themselves off...they got into an animated conversation...animated means lots of waving about of hands and tossing your head back and that kind of thing. And the outcome was that the woman realized this man was the Messiah! She started jumping up and down with excitement…she hugged Jesus…and told him to wait there…and she ran over to the service counter…grabbed the microphone for the store intercom…and shouted…I've found Jesus!…On aisle three!…Free living water!…Hurry over!

And not satisfied with that, she dug her cell phone out of her purse…still digging…and called the first person on speed dial…and shouted into the phone…Get over to the grocery store!… Jesus is here!…He told me everything I ever did!…Yes…I know what I've done… Yes…I know you know, too…But never mind that! Bring everyone you know!

She called everyone on her speed dial that day…and people streamed to the store to see Jesus, who waved wildly… wildly…to everyone. Jesus stayed for two days, and many people believed in him.

Say: *OK, it probably wasn't exactly like this…but you get the idea! This woman didn't just quietly hear the news Jesus shared with her and then sneak back home. She wanted to get the word out! She wanted everyone to know Jesus.*

Continue with your session.

Spiritual Growth

We all desire spiritual growth in ourselves, and in the people around us. And God has provided us tools such as the Bible, fellowship, and prayer. Use this warm-up to introduce a discussion on spiritual growth and the tools necessary for true growth.

Prep and Supplies

- a bowl or bag of potting soil

- spade

- pruning shears or scissors

- a watering can with water in it

- seeds (sunflower seeds work well because they're large and available all year)

Place these items on tables around the room, with one item per table. This warm-up will move more smoothly if you write the discussion questions out and place a copy by each item or post them in a visible place in the front of the room.

The Warm-Up

Encourage women to pair up and walk around the room to each gardening tool or item. Once they get to a specific tool or supply, ask them to discuss the following questions in regards to that item. Then have pairs move to the next tool or item and discuss the questions again in regards to that item.

Tip

This warm-up works well with Psalm 92:11-13 or John 15:1-3.

- *Why is this tool or supply important to gardening and the growth of a plant?*

- *When you think of spiritual growth, what "spiritual" tool or supply is most like this gardening one?*

- *Why is that spiritual tool or supply important to spiritual growth?*

- *How has God used that spiritual tool in your life?*

Allow at least 10 minutes for this warm-up. It's OK if women don't make it to every item—they should have had time to consider and discuss a few of them when you call time and have everyone return to their seats so you can continue your session.

Temptation

Everyone faces temptation every day. Use this warm-up to help women recognize the temptations they face, and to discuss how they rely on God to defeat those temptations.

The Warm-Up

Encourage women to look at all the different ads you've placed on the table. After women have looked for a little while, have everyone choose one ad that represents the thing that's most tempting to them. It's fine if some women want to choose the same ads, just have them sit down next to each other for the discussion.

After everyone is sitting down again, have women form small groups of no more than five. Have each woman share in her group which ad she chose and why the thing represented is tempting to her. Have groups discuss the following questions together:

- *On a daily basis, what temptations do you face?*
- *How do you have victory over them?*
- *What do you do when they have victory over you?*

Continue your session, being sure to include how God can help us avoid those temptations!

Prep and Supplies

- current magazines

Before your meeting, cut out several magazine ads for different products—anything from chocolate to shoes to clothing to cars. Spread all the ads out on a table or several tables.

Tip

This warm-up works well with 1 Corinthians 10:13.

Trust

Use this activity to get women ready for a session on learning to trust God.

Prep and Supplies

NO PREP

The Warm-Up

Have women form groups of four. Ask each woman to find the most valuable thing that she has with her. This might be an heirloom piece of jewelry she's wearing, a picture of her child, a credit card…anything that she feels is most valuable.

Have women share in their groups about these items, showing them to the others and then telling about them. Then ask each woman to give her item to the woman on her right, who will hold it in her hand for now.

Ask: *How do you feel about letting go of this item for a short while?*

Let women talk about that in their groups, and then continue with your session. Don't have women return the items to their owners until the very end of your session. You might want to wrap up this session with a follow-up question about how hard or easy it was for women to let that item stay out of their control for that much time.

Unity/Community/ Body of Christ

The Bible regularly uses the body as a metaphor for the church, and what a perfect metaphor! The body is precise in its detail and coordination. The smallest movement takes the cooperation of many parts. Use this warm-up to discuss the metaphor further.

Prep and Supplies

• 1 picture of the anatomy of a hand or a foot per five women

You can find pictures like this online at medical sites. Make sure all the parts are labeled, and, if possible, print out a description of each part.

Tip

This warm-up works well with 1 Corinthians 12.

The Warm-Up

Have women get into groups of about five and give each group a picture of the anatomy of a hand or foot. As it's being passed, have different women read off descriptions of each part of the hand or foot, and how that part works with the whole. After women have looked at the picture and read the descriptions, have them discuss these questions in their groups:

• What struck you as we looked at the hand [or foot] and listened to the descriptions?

• There is so much intricate detail to how the body works together. How is that like or unlike our church community?

• How does our church work together like a body? How can we do better?

• What part do you play in the body of our group? In the body of our church?

Continue with your session.

Wisdom

Get women interested in the topic of wisdom with this creative activity.

Prep and Supplies

- index cards
- pens or pencils

The Warm-Up

Give each woman two index cards and a pen or pencil.

Say: *You've certainly heard old "proverbs" or sayings such as "A bird in the hand is worth two in the bush," or "An apple a day keeps the doctor away." I'd like you to think of a couple of proverbs that would be helpful for women today. These can be funny or serious, or you might want to update an old saying like, "A bird in the hand should be boneless, skinless, and ready to cook." Write whatever short saying of wisdom you think a woman today should keep in mind.*

Allow several minutes for women to be creative. If anyone complains that she's "stuck" and just can't think of anything, have women work in pairs or groups of three and encourage them to work together on this fun and creative exercise.

Gather the cards, and read as many aloud as time permits. There are certain to be a few funny ones, and some that will make women nod in agreement. Then ask:

- *As you listened to these, what were common themes or bits of wisdom you noticed?*

- *What was one new proverb that stood out to you most, and why?*

Continue your session on wisdom.

Worry

Worry weighs a person down and an encouraging word lifts a person up. This warm-up demonstrates physically how women feel emotionally when we worry and how encouraging words can relieve that burden.

The Warm-Up

Have women form groups of four or five, and ask each woman to pick up one heavy item and bring it back to her seat.

Say: *Think of something you're likely to worry about. Go around your group and say that worry as you hold your item out in front of you. Extend your arms and hold it out there without bending your arms—no cheating!*

Allow about two minutes—those items will start to get heavy! Then have women go around the circle again, and say that same worry, but this time add that worry to the arms of the woman wearing the most red. See if she can hang onto these worries even for 30 seconds! Then have women put all their "worries" on their laps and discuss these questions in their small groups:

- *What physical reaction did your body have to the weight of your worry?*
- *When do you feel most weighed down by worry?*
- *How did your feelings change when the burden began to come off?*
- *How can encouragement from someone else lift your burden of worry?*

Continue with your session.

Prep and Supplies

- large rocks, bricks, weights, books or other heavy objects that can be added one by one

Place your heavy items around the room so women can have access to them.

Tip

This warm-up works well with Proverbs 12:25.

Wrap-Ups

Balance

This wrap-up demonstrates how difficult balancing the many aspects of our lives can be without God's direction.

The Wrap-Up

Say: *We've been discussing balance and how God needs to be a part of helping us find the right balance in our lives. Let's try an activity that will help us get a better picture of what that balance should look like.*

Invite two or three women to join you in the front of the room.

First, time how fast these women can stack the blocks. See who can stack the most without letting any fall in 30 seconds.

Next, blindfold each of your volunteers and repeat the activity. How many can be stacked in 30 seconds with a blindfold on?

After completing this activity, thank your volunteers and discuss the following questions in smaller groups:

- *What differences did you observe or experience between these balancing acts?*

- *How is having God a part of balancing our lives like or unlike balancing the blocks without the blindfold?*

- *What's one way you could involve God in creating balance in your life this week?*

Give each woman one of the blocks, and have her write her answer to the last question on that block. Encourage women to take these home and put them where they'll be seen every day as a reminder to keep God involved in finding balance in their lives.

Prep and Supplies

- toy blocks (wood or plastic)
- blindfolds (dishtowels or bandanas work great)
- watch or clock with second hand

Tip

If you have enough blocks, have women form pairs and do this together, taking turns timing each other. It's a lot of fun when everyone gets to participate—but you do need a big supply of blocks!

Beauty

Prep and Supplies

- several colors of nail polish (you'll need to include a few bottles of sparkly glitter polish, too)
- cotton balls
- nail polish remover
- old magazines or newspapers

Tip

This wrap-up uses Isaiah 52:7.

This wrap-up gives women a tangible challenge to consider and pursue the true beauty which God desires for them.

The Wrap-Up

As you close your session on beauty, read Isaiah 52:7 aloud.

Ask: *What new perspective does this verse give you on the concept of beauty?*

After a few women have shared their thoughts, invite women to take off their shoes and paint their toenails. Women are not *required* to paint their nails—but do set a good example by joining in yourself!

Make sure everyone has access to supplies, and use the magazines or newspapers to place on the floor so women won't spill polish or remover on the flooring.

As the women work on their toes, encourage them to discuss with someone sitting nearby what sharing *the good news of peace and salvation* looks like in their neighborhood, school, or workplace. This sharing can be as light as mentioning to a neighbor what a refreshing time they had at a recent women's retreat or as deep as sharing the story of their own salvation with a babysitter. Encourage women to think of *particular* people in their circles with whom they can share good news during the coming week.

Invite each woman to coat one toe with the glittery polish as a reminder to pursue Christ-like beauty by sharing good news with those around her. Suggest that women refrain from removing their glittery toe polish until they have found an opportunity to share good news with a neighbor or acquaintance.

Contentment

In today's world, contentment can be hard to come by. New cars, new clothes, new houses. The Joneses. It's a world of more, more, more—and it's hard to stay satisfied. Use this wrap-up to challenge women to explore their areas of discontent and to counter them with gratitude, realistic expectations, and knowledge of their true identity in God.

Prep and Supplies

- copies of the questions for reflection
- pens or pencils

Tip

This wrap-up works well with Philippians 4:11-13.

The Wrap-Up

As you draw your meeting to a close, encourage women to scatter throughout the building for about 10 minutes of reflection. Provide copies of these questions for them to use as they evaluate their own lives.

- *Where are you the least content in your life?*
- *What are you most content with in your life?*
- *What are the differences between that and the area you are least content?*
- *What are you most grateful for in your life?*
- *How can gratitude help you deal with your discontent?*

After about 10 minutes, have women come together and share with a partner one thing they'll do this week as a result of what they decided in this time of reflection.

Forgiveness

When God forgives our wrongdoings, we have a fresh and clean start. This wrap-up will leave women feeling a sense of God's cleansing forgiveness.

The Wrap-Up

Say: *God wants us to learn to forgive, because it's part of God's nature to be forgiving. Let's experience what God's forgiveness feels like.*

Form pairs and have women remove rings, watches, or bracelets. Squirt a quarter-sized dollop of clay facial mask on each woman's hands. Direct women to smooth the clay over their hands and allow it to dry. While women allow the clay to dry, have them discuss the following questions with a partner:

- *What is a sin you need God to forgive?*

- *How is that sin like this clay on your hands?*

Read 1 John 1:9 aloud. Then have partners wash each other's hands and dry them. As they do, encourage women to tell their partners, "[Name], God will forgive you."

Prep and Supplies

- container of clay facial mask
- a few buckets or pitchers of water
- paper towels

Tip

This activity uses 1 John 1:9.

Tip

Let women know that they don't need to share their deepest, darkest secrets. You may want to share something like "Gossip" or "Losing my temper" to help others feel comfortable sharing things they're struggling with.

Friendship

This wrap-up gives women the opportunity to express their gratitude for a friendship.

Prep and Supplies

- empty cereal boxes

- heavy scissors

- local phonebook or church directory

- pens

- 1 postage stamp per woman

If you're feeling particularly festive you can also include some fun stickers. Note, you don't need to have *eaten* all that cereal. Just leave the inner bag in your cupboard!

The Wrap-Up

Begin by inviting each woman in the group to think of a friend, not in the group, for whom she is grateful.

Next, invite women to choose a cereal box from which they will cut out a postcard to mail to that friend. Women may want to include a word from the packaging that describes the friendship such as "wholesome," "body-building," or "crunchy."

Encourage women to share what is meaningful about their friendship in the note they write on their postcard. Then have women share what they've written with a partner nearby—after all, if the mail carrier can read it, it can certainly be shared with the group!

If there's a mailbox in the neighborhood, take a short walk together and say a quick prayer for each friend as you mail the postcards.

Tip

The smallest size postcard accepted by the United States Postal Service is 3.5 x 5-inch and the largest is 4.25 x 6-inch. Larger sizes than that will require additional postage.

Gentleness

Words can be harsh or gently healing. This wrap-up challenges women to use gentle words.

Prep and Supplies

- small square of a soft, silky fabric per person
- small square of rough sandpaper per person

Tip

This wrap-up works well with Colossians 3:12.

The Wrap-Up

Have women form groups of four or five, and give each person one piece of the silky fabric and one piece of the sandpaper.

Say: *Hold the sandpaper in your hand, and as you rub your fingers over that, take turns going around your group and say words that describe that sandpaper. Continue until you can't think of any more descriptive words.*

Allow several minutes for groups to share, and then have a few people share some of the words their group expressed.

Say: *Silently think of someone who could be described by the words you've said aloud. Perhaps someone who is rough, abrasive, scratchy. The person might even be you! You don't have to say the name of this person aloud, just think about that person for a minute and reflect on what this person does that makes you associate these scratchy words with him or her.*

Allow a minute for reflection. Then say: *Now hold the silky fabric in your hand. As you rub your fingers over this, take turns going around your group and saying words that describe this fabric. Again, continue until you can't think of more descriptive words.*

Allow a few minutes for sharing, then draw women's attention to you and comment on the similarities to these words and the subject of gentleness that you've been discussing.

Say: *Now I'd like you to think about what it would take for other people to describe you with those gentle words. You don't have to share aloud, but I would like you to take a minute to think about the words you've heard. Do others use those words to describe you? Are you a gentle person, soft, soothing, enjoyable to be around? What would it take to become a gentle person? Think on these things for a minute.*

When time is up, encourage women to take the two materials home and place them where they can be seen as a reminder of what it means to be gentle.

God's Plan/God's Will

This wrap-up gives women a chance to consider how God is using them, and what part they play in his plan.

Prep and Supplies

- various tools and instruments such as an iron, shovel, a musical instrument or two, a measuring cup, and so on. You should have at least 10 different items.

Place the items in a very visible area, such as on a table in the front of the room.

The Wrap-Up

As you begin to wrap-up your session, draw women's attention to the tools and instruments you've placed on the table. Hold up each one in turn so women can see what they are.

Explain that you'd like each woman to choose one item that she thinks best illustrates how God is using her as a part of his plan, based on what you've already shared in your session. For example, one person might choose a shovel because she thinks her purpose right now is to dig deeper into relationships with teens in her community. Another might choose a harmonica to represent her desire to be a voice for change. Encourage women to be creative as they consider the items—the same item might be chosen by more than one person for entirely different reasons.

Allow a few minutes for women to consider the tools and instruments. If space permits, let them get up and walk around the table where the items are displayed. Then have each person find a partner and tell what item she chose, and what it represents to her. Use this as an affirmation that God has a purpose and a plan for using each of us as *his* instruments.

Goodness

This wrap-up will challenge women to think of ways they can put "doing good" into action.

Prep and Supplies

NO PREP

Tip

This activity uses Galatians 6:9-10.

The Wrap-Up

Have women find partners, and then read Galatians 6:9-10 aloud.

Ask the following questions, one at a time. After each question allow about three minutes for women to talk with their partners about their responses, and then ask the next question.

Ask: *When have you felt worn-down in doing good?*

- *How does this verse encourage you to continue in doing good?*

- *What opportunities do you have to put this verse into action this week? Be specific!*

Have a few of the pairs share their ideas for putting the verse into action to close your time together. Encourage partners to exchange their contact information so they can hold each other accountable this coming week.

Grace

Tip

This warm-up works well with Psalm 34:8.

Prep and Supplies

- 1 chocolate bar per woman
- markers
- colorful paper
- tape
- stickers (optional)

Women will be using the supplies to make a new wrapper for their chocolate bars. Cut the paper to the proper size so women will be able to quickly make new wrappers. Place the supplies in various locations around the room. You might want to make one ahead of time to show as a sample.

Tip

Since you're using the chocolate as a symbol of God's extravagant grace, don't skimp on quality! Get a good brand of chocolate.

God's grace is a lot like chocolate—it's sweet, extravagant, and the perfect gift. This wrap-up uses chocolate as a gift of grace to someone else.

The Wrap-Up

Say: *As we've considered God's grace and what it means in our lives, I'd like us to think of chocolate as a symbol of God's lavish and extravagant grace. It's sweet, extravagant, and an undeserved gift.*

One way we might reflect God's grace and celebrate his gift to us is by giving a gracious gift to someone else. I've created a new wrapper for this bar of chocolate so I can give it as a gift. It's a small way I can celebrate God's grace to me—by giving a gift to someone else. We're going to

take time now for each person to create a chocolate bar wrapper to give to someone else. Perhaps yours will be a gift to convey the joy of a friendship. Or it might be a way of expressing thanks or be an invitation to join you in learning more about God. It's up to you, but use your creativity and the supplies I've provided to lavish a tiny bit of love and grace on someone else.

Direct women to the supplies you've set out and let them use their creativity to make a gift for someone. Allow about 10 minutes for this, and encourage women to tell someone sitting nearby about the friend they are going to give this gift to and why.

Hope

This wrap-up focuses on putting our hope in God.

Prep and Supplies

- 1 birthday candle per person
- 1 cupcake per person
- matches or a lighter

Tip

This activity works well with Psalm 110:147 or Psalm 130:5.

The Wrap-Up

Say: *One fun birthday ritual is blowing out the candles on the birthday cake and making a wish for the next year. As adults we don't believe our wishes will come true, but we do sometimes think that "if only" something would change, our lives would be so much better. "If only I could get a new job. . ." "If only I could lose weight. . ." "If only I could find the perfect man…" Turn to someone sitting beside you and share what you're most likely to say, "If only" about.*

Allow a minute or two for discussion, then read Psalm 130:5 or 110:147 aloud.

Say: *Think about these verses. Where is your hope? Is it in the Lord or is it in an "if only"?*

Give each person a cupcake and candle.

Say: *We're going to light, and then blow out, our candles. As you blow out your candle, let it symbolize blowing out the things you've put your hope in other than God and a decision to put your hope in him instead.*

Light the candles, have everyone blow them out together, and celebrate your hope in God with a sweet treat!

Integrity

God calls us to have integrity—to live so people can see him in our lives. This wrap-up will give women the opportunity to encourage each other to live with integrity.

Prep and Supplies

- permanent markers

- 1 disposable, clear, plastic cup per woman

- 1 solid-colored tumbler that you can't see through

Fill the tumbler halfway with a snack or liquid.

The Wrap-Up

Hold up the solid-colored cup and allow women to guess what's inside. After 30 seconds (or when someone guesses correctly), say: *A cup like this can hold anything. You can't tell just by looking at it what's inside. But God wants us to be transparent—to show others his incredible love in all we do. As a woman living a life of integrity, you might look more like this!* Hold up a clear cup. Ask women to think of the things that should be easy to see in our lives and call some of those out loud.

Distribute cups and permanent markers. Allow five minutes for women to write those words on each other's cups, as an affirmation to let others see Christ in all we do.

Tip

This activity goes well with Proverbs 27:19.

Joy

Our joy in Christ should be evident through our lives. This wrap-up gives a visual illustration of overflowing joy when our lives are filled with the Holy Spirit.

Prep and Supplies

- 1 disposable, plastic cup per woman
- 1 drinking straw per woman
- Joy dish-washing liquid
- water
- towels or paper towels

Tip

This activity works well with Romans 15:13.

The Wrap-Up

Give each woman a disposable cup filled with water, and a drinking straw.

Say: *Remember when you were a kid and you would use a straw to blow bubbles in a glass of milk? Well let's try that again using these glasses of water.*

Have women put the straws into the water and blow—making bubbles. (This is where you might want those towels or paper towels). After a minute, ask: *What about those bubbles? Are any of them remaining?* Clearly, the bubbles disappear as soon as the blowing stops.

Now pass around *Joy* dishwashing liquid and have each woman squeeze a bit into her water. Let the bubble-blowing begin. (Again…you might want those towels!) After a minute ask:

- *What's different this time?*
- *What makes joy bubble up and last in our lives, instead of just disappearing?*

Encourage women to use the principles you've shared to make the joy of Jesus bubble up and overflow continuously, instead of just once in a while.

Kindness

An act of kindness can change a day. It's refreshing and invigorating for everyone involved. Use this wrap-up as a time for women to commit to acts of kindness during the upcoming week.

Prep and Supplies

- a glass of cold water per woman
- pens or pencils
- paper

Tip

This wrap-up works really well with Philemon 1:7.

The Wrap-Up

Give each woman a glass of cold water. Remind everyone that kindness is refreshing—to those that receive it, and those that give it. Have women write down the names of five or six people in their lives; family members, co-workers, neighbors—just anyone they think of. Then have women close their eyes and think about one way they can be kind to each person on their list. After they think of each person, encourage women to take a refreshing sip of water. Once all the women have gone through their list, have them pair up and discuss the following questions:

- *What acts of kindness did you think of doing?*
- *How might those actions be refreshing to that person? To you?*
- *How has God's kindness changed your life?*
- *How can you live with an attitude of kindness even after this week?*

Wrap-Ups

Loneliness

Many times women feel lonely and focus only on themselves—forgetting that others are lonely too. This warm-up takes action on reaching out to another who needs a friend.

Prep and Supplies

- attractive note cards with matching envelopes
- pens

The Wrap-Up

As you draw your session on loneliness to a close, remind women that they are not alone in feeling lonely. Many women feel exactly the same way and long for someone to reach out to them.

Have each woman think of at least one person she knows that might be lonely. This could be just about anyone! Distribute the note cards, envelopes, and pens, and have each person write a note to the person she thought of. This could be a note with a verse in it, a bit of encouragement, a thanks for friendship, or anything that is uplifting and says, "I like you!"

Ask women to commit to mailing or delivering these cards within two days, and to pray for one week for the person they are sending the card to, asking that God would bring more friends to her life, and would comfort her in times of loneliness.

Love

When we are loving to others, it's like the beautiful aroma of flowers—not overpowering, but noticeable. This wrap-up encourages women to put love into action with a simple, aromatic gift.

Prep and Supplies

- 1 small sachet of dried flower petals per woman

Tip

You can make these sachets easily by filling a small organza bag with about 1/3 cup of dried flower petals that you've added a few drops of flower oil to. Then just pull the drawstrings on the bag and you've got a little sachet.

The Wrap-Up

Give each woman one of the sachets.

Say: *We've been talking about love and what it means to be loving in our actions to others. Actions of love can be like the aroma of flowers—beautiful and attractive, but not overpowering or off-putting.*

These sachets are filled with dried flower petals that still are giving off a beautiful fragrance. Take a whiff right now! I'd like you to think of someone you can share God's love with this week through words or actions. Give this person this gift of fragrance as a starting point, and then find one other way to spread God's love through your friendship with that person.

Have each person find a partner and tell who she is going to share God's love with this week, and how. After about five minutes, have women hold their sachets in their hands as they pray for the person they will be sharing love with that week.

Obedience

One way we can show our love for God is to obey him. This wrap-up challenges women to grow in obedience.

Prep and Supplies

- paper
- pens or pencils

Tip

This wrap-up uses John 14:21.

The Wrap-Up

Have women form small groups of three or four. Provide pens and paper, and have groups list as many laws as they can, along with the consequences for breaking that law.

After a few minutes, have groups share a few of their laws and the consequences for breaking that law. Then ask groups to discuss:

- *Why would you, or anyone, not obey a law?*

After a few minutes of discussion, let a few women share what was discussed in their groups. Use this as a time to point out that we might disobey laws because we don't believe they're important or we don't respect those who made the laws. Read John 14:21 aloud, and ask women to discuss:

- *How does obedience show love?*

After a few minutes of discussion, have a few women share with the entire group. Use their answers as a challenge for everyone to consider obedience in ways to express love for Jesus.

Patience

A day in the life of a woman can bring many occasions for showing patience. Use this wrap-up as a time for women to demonstrate patience as they think through ways to be patient in the upcoming week.

The Wrap-Up

Prep and Supplies

- 1 ice cube per woman

Tip

This wrap-up works well with Proverbs 19:11; 14:29, or 15:18.

Give every woman in your group an ice cube to hold in their hands. It's going to get cold! But encourage women to hold the ice cube tightly until it melts. Yup, patience will be required. As they hold the ice, have them think about the upcoming week and all the ways their patience will be tried. Encourage them to consider ways they can counter that impatience: through prayer, deep breaths, kind words, and so on.

As the ice melts, remind women that patience is tough, sometimes painful…but it always melts away a tense situation and drains the anger from everyone involved.

After a few minutes, throw away any remaining ice cubes and encourage women to pair up and discuss the following questions:

- *When do you expect your patience to be tried this week?*
- *How will you fight impatience in that situation?*
- *How has God been patient with you?*
- *Why is it important to mirror that patience in your own life?*

Peace

With the pressure of juggling different roles, women often find that peace is hard to find. Use this wrap-up to remind women that they can find peace by giving their burdens to Jesus.

Prep and Supplies

Before the session, hide a five-dollar bill somewhere in the room. It should be hidden so that no one can see it, but can easily be found.

Tip

This wrap-up uses Matthew 11:28-30.

The Wrap-Up

Explain that you've hidden something in the room that's desirable to everyone and a gift to the one who finds it. Give the group a few minutes to find what you've hidden, encouraging everyone to get out of their chairs and look around. As they search, talk about how peace is sometimes hard to find, but if we look for it we can find it.

After the money has been found, have women form small groups of three or four and share:

• *What does it take for you to find peace?*

• *Is peace valuable to you and worth finding? Why or why not?*

Then read Matthew 11:28-30 aloud. Talk about how we lose sight of peace when we take on burdens that God isn't asking us to carry. Explain how peace, like the five dollars, is always there and available to us if we're willing to put first things first in our lives.

Pride

Pride can keep us from building friendships, serving others, and serving God. Use this wrap-up to encourage women to let go of pride that might be holding them back.

Prep and Supplies

- 4 uninflated balloons per woman

The Wrap-Up

Give each woman at least four balloons.

Say: *When someone is proud, we might say he or she has a "big head" or an "inflated ego." So let's inflate some egos...I mean, balloons!*

Have women inflate and tie off each balloon. As women do this, encourage them to silently think of a specific area of pride in their own lives. Women might identify things such as "looks," "friendships," or "clothing." When the balloons are all inflated, ask women to hold all of their balloons in their arms or hands, and join hands to form a circle. Ask:

- *How do the balloons keep you from connecting with each other?*

- *How does pride keep us from connecting with each other?*

Say: *Let's get rid of all these inflated egos!* Let women creatively pop their balloons, then join hands and close in prayer. Ask God to keep pride out of our lives so we can develop strong, lasting friendships...with others *and* with God.

Purity

Sometimes temptation comes in the form of huge life-destroying seductions and mistakes. But the more prevalent (and perhaps more powerful) temptation comes through the small, constant, almost gnat-like voices and images that chip away at the purity of our hearts. Use this devotion to encourage women to guard their hearts and minds against the messages that seek to break their resolve, peace, and purity.

Prep and Supplies

- 1 white paper heart per woman
- 1 red paper heart per woman
- dark crayons
- glue sticks

Tip

This activity uses Philippians 4:8.

The Wrap-Up

Have women use crayons to write on their white hearts all the things they can think of that might take away their purity and fill their minds or bodies with impurity. After a few minutes, comment on the fact that like the crayon, these cannot be erased. They stick in our minds and make it hard to keep pure.

Read Philippians 4:8, and ask women to consider this verse a challenge as they leave today. Remind them that the blood of Jesus can cover our sins and make us pure again. Have women glue a red heart over their white heart as a reminder of this.

Purpose

This wrap-up gives women a chance to consider their own purpose and to recognize and affirm one another's gifts.

Prep and Supplies

- index cards
- pens or pencils
- a doll or action figure. This could be a child's baby doll, a large rag doll or even a plastic action figure. Because all the women in the circle will want to see it, bigger is better.

Tip

If you have more than 10 women in your group, bring a few extra dolls and form smaller groups so there's time for each person to be affirmed.

The Wrap-Up

As you've been discussing purpose, point out that others might see purpose in us that we don't see in ourselves. Give everyone a few index cards, and have everyone sit in a circle. Hand the doll to one person.

Say: *As [Name] holds the doll, I'd like each of you to write down which body part on the doll expresses how you see her functioning. It might be how you see her functioning here in our group, in her home, in her place of work, or anywhere you've observed her. And, the person holding the doll should write down one body part as well.*

Encourage creativity by reminding women that someone could be a spleen, eyelash, or red corpuscle just as well as a foot, hand, or nose.

Beginning with the woman at the doll-holder's left, invite each one to read her word and explain it. Continue around the circle, having the woman holding the doll share her own thoughts last. Then gather these cards and give them to the woman with the doll as an affirmation she can keep. Then pass the doll to the next woman and continue until each person has been affirmed. Use this time to affirm that God has a unique purpose for each woman, even if she doesn't see it in herself.

Self-Control

Wrap-Ups

Sometimes laughter can give us the strength to use self-control. This fun wrap-up will give women a silly mental picture to encourage them to use restraint.

Prep and Supplies

- balloons or scrap paper

- a girdle (the more outlandish the better!)

Tip

If you have a large group, form trios and give each trio a pair of support-top nylons. Let trios stuff them... legs and all!

The Wrap-Up

Hold up the girdle and say: *Sometimes, self-control means holding it in! Let's stuff this "control top" with all the things in our lives that require self-control.*

Let women inflate balloons (halfway) or crumple up scrap paper. Each time they do, have them say something that requires self-control, then stuff the balloon or paper wad into the girdle. Continue until the girdle is full.

Talk about how humor can give us the strength to use self-control in different situations. Encourage women to keep the visual of the "stuffed girdle" in mind when they need some help with self-control.

Service

Actions speak louder than words. This wrap-up demonstrates, to and through women, that Christ's love is seen clearly through their service to others.

Prep and Supplies

- bottles of window cleaner

- rags or paper towels

The Wrap-Up

As you've been talking with women about service, let them know it's time to put the discussion into action. Women will move outside and wash car windows.

If your group meets in a public space or a bustling residential neighborhood, women can target cars of strangers or other church members. If you meet in a more isolated location, women can wash the windows of each another's vehicles, or those of a family member of the hostess. Or, if you have concerns about car alarms, knock on the door of a nearby home or business and ask for permission to wash the outside of their building windows!

As the women work side by side, invite them to reflect on this question:

- *Have you ever experienced Christ's love for you through the service of someone else? If so, how?*

Encourage women to think of other ways that Christ's love can be expressed through service opportunities that naturally present themselves within the daily fabric of their lives.

Sharing Your Faith

Thanking those who have shared their faith with us can encourage us to share our faith with others. This wrap-up allows women to tell their own stories as means of encouraging others to share their faith.

Prep and Supplies

NO PREP

The Wrap-Up

As you draw your time of discussing sharing your faith to a close, have women form groups of four or five. Ask each woman to tell about someone who shared their faith in Jesus with her and what that meant to her. This might be the story of how each woman became a Christian, or it might be the story of a step along the way in that journey.

Allow at least 15 minutes so each woman has a few minutes to share her story. Then challenge women to consider the different ways that they and others in the room heard about Jesus. It's likely that no two stories are alike! Challenge women to use the stories of others as encouragement, that they can take the simple steps, just like others before them, to share their faith.

Spiritual Growth

This wrap-up uses real and artificial flowers as a tangible reminder of what it means to be growing in faith.

The Wrap-Up

Have women get into groups of four or five. Ask one person from each group to select a real and an artificial flower and take those back to her group. Encourage women to touch, smell, and closely examine their flowers as they discuss these two questions together:

- *How are your two flowers alike?*
- *How are your two flowers different?*

Allow five to 10 minutes for discussion, and have a few groups report back their findings. Note that the key difference really comes down to the fact that one flower is living, and the other is not. Remind the women of the things you've shared in your session that keep us alive and growing spiritually. You might want to have women share in their groups one thing they'll do this week to stay alive, fresh, fragrant, and blooming in their friendship with Jesus.

Prep and Supplies

- a variety of real flowers and artificial ones

Place the flowers in vases about the room where women will have easy access to them. Place the artificial ones in different vases than the real ones so women can choose one of each quickly.

Tip

Fabric flowers will work better for this activity than plastic ones.

Temptation

Whether it was Eve in the garden or Jesus in the wilderness, the deceiver's signature temptation is to entice us into taking matters into our own hands. This wrap-up teaches this timeless truth in a memorable way.

The Wrap-Up

As you are wrapping up your study or discussion of temptation, ask women to silently reflect on this question:

- *When are you tempted to take things into your own hands?*

Explain that this question is very broad: it could mean being over-controlling or it might mean reaching for false substitutes such as a drink, a pill, or a piece of cake. Give everyone a few moments to reflect silently.

Then have women move to the tables and make a fingerprint on at least two index cards. Women can do more if they want.

Say: *Beside each fingerprint, write something you can reach for with your hands when you're tempted to take things into your own hands. It might be a Bible, the telephone to call a friend, a journal, or something else.*

Allow a few minutes for women to write on several cards. Encourage women to share at least one of their cards with a partner, and tell what she wants to reach for instead of taking the situation into her own hands.

Women can take the cards home as a reminder of their commitment—and the ink that is hard to get off of their fingers will be a good reminder for at least a few hours, too!

Prep and Supplies

- index cards
- ink pads
- pens or pencils
- wet wipes

Place these items on tables around the room so women can move there and have easy access to using them.

Tip

This is a good wrap-up for a study on Matthew 4:1-11 or Genesis 3.

Trust

This wrap-up uses a tried and true method to remind women of what it's like to trust others—and to be trusted.

Prep and Supplies

- soft, cloth blindfolds

The Wrap-Up

As you bring your study of trust to a close, have each person find a partner.

Say: *We've probably all heard about trust walks, where one person leads a blindfolded person around. Some of you might have done one at some time in your lives. It's an experience worth repeating as it really helps us apply what we're learning about trust.*

Have the shorter person in each pair put on a blindfold, and ask the taller person to lead her around for at least five minutes. Encourage women to walk outdoors, up or down stairs, through colder or warmer areas, and so on. You might even set up areas with fans, heaters, loud noises, and so on to make the experience more memorable.

After five minutes have partners switch roles, and then have everyone return to your meeting area. Discuss these questions:

- *Was it easier for you to trust, or be trusted? Explain.*

- *As you compare this activity to your everyday life, are you more likely to trust others or to expect others to trust you?*

- *How does trusting God fit into your everyday life?*

Unity/Community/ Body of Christ

Growing together, living together, serving together. God calls us to unity as a body of Christians. Use this wrap-up experience to help women discover a sense of community.

The Wrap-Up

Have women form groups of about seven or eight, and stand in a circle with their arms around the women on either side—like a huddle. Be sure women are standing at least two feet away from chairs or tables.

Say: *Close your eyes. Silently reflect and respond to the thoughts I share.*

We enjoy fellowship…laughing together, serving together, growing together. Being together feels great! But sometimes we get selfish. If you've ever been selfish, thinking of and acting for yourself, drop your arms. (Pause.)

Sometimes we say things that separate us from others, and we can't enjoy the love God intends for us. If you've ever hurt someone with your words, take one step back from the circle. (Pause.)

Even though we're the body of Christ, sometimes we turn on members of that body. If you've ever turned your back on someone in need, turn away from the circle. (Pause.)

God never turns his back on us. He forgives us, calling us back. If you've been forgiven for a wrongdoing, turn back toward the circle. (Pause.)

United in Christ, we can do incredible things for God. If you've ever had someone serve you with the love of Jesus, take a step forward. (Pause.)

As the body of Christ, we rely on each other. We comfort each other. We reach out to each other. If someone has ever reached out to you, put your arms around the women on either side of you. (Pause.)

Close in prayer, asking God to help you act as the body of Christ, united in perfect love.

Wisdom

When someone is wise, you might say, "She's got a good head on her shoulders." Use this fun wrap-up to allow women to share words of wisdom.

Prep and Supplies

- markers
- tape
- 1 sheet of paper per woman
- CD player and CD of upbeat music

The Wrap-Up

Distribute the markers and paper, and allow each woman to draw her face on a sheet of paper. Tape the pictures around the room. Explain that when a woman is wise, we say she's got a good head on her shoulders…and your group is filled with "good heads."

Play upbeat music and allow women to visit each picture and write a few words of wisdom on the picture. Encourage women to make their words of wisdom specific for each group member, rather than simply repeating one phrase for the group. Women may write a prayer or a verse, or share some Christian insight to that person's life.

After about 10 minutes, let women silently read the wisdom that's been shared, and then have each woman take her own picture down and take it home as a reminder of the wisdom and encouragement others have shared with her.

Worry

Worry can tie us up in knots! This activity will help women discover that God can untangle those worries.

Prep and Supplies

- a 12-inch length of string for each woman

Tip

This activity uses Matthew 6:25-33.

The Wrap-Up

Give each woman a length of string and direct women to form groups of no more than four.

Say: *Sometimes, worries can tie us up in knots. Share a few of your worries with your small group. For each worry, tie a knot in your string.*

Allow about five minutes for women to share. Then read aloud Matthew 6:25-33.

Say: *God's Word tells us not to worry. So hand your worry knots to someone else in the group. Untie your friend's worries and talk about ways you've seen God take away worries in your life. Encourage each other. You may even have a bit of Scripture that will help one of your group members with one of her worries.*

Play upbeat music while women share with and encourage each other…and untie all those worrisome knots!

Prayers

Balance

This prayer reminds women that leaning on God and others is a great way to find balance.

Prep and Supplies

NO PREP

The Prayer

Have women form groups of no more than five and stand in small circles with their groups. Have each woman put her hands onto the shoulders of those beside her, and then stand on one foot. Women can use the stability of the circle to remain balanced.

Say: *As you balance together, talk to God about the areas of your lives where you need more balance. Thank God for friends who help you stay balanced, or maybe ask God to provide friends who will bring more balance into your life.*

Prayers

Beauty

This prayer encourages women to focus on inner beauty.

Prep and Supplies

• 1 small mirror for each woman

The Prayer

Give each woman a small mirror, and have her hold it in front of her face, reflecting her own image to herself.

Say: *We're going to pray silently as we look at ourselves in our mirrors. We may look at ourselves and see beauty—or we may be critical of what we see. But God sees deeper.*

As I mention features on our faces, thank God for that beautiful part of your face, and ask him to use it for his beautiful purposes. For example, you might thank God for your eyes, and then pray that they would see others in need, or that they would look for signs of God's grace every day.

As you say each of the following features, wait at least one minute for women to silently pray, thanking God for that part of her and asking him to use it for a beautiful purpose. Mention eyes, nose, lips, ears, teeth.

Prayers

Contentment

Too often we're enticed by what we don't have, and feel discontent. This prayer encourages women to practice gratitude for the ways the Lord *has* been gracious to meet their needs.

Prep and Supplies

- pens or pencils
- paper
- CD player and CD of soft music

The Prayer

Invite women to write lists of things that they feel unhappy or discontented about. This might be feeling bad that they didn't get to take a fun vacation this year, that they long for a better job, they wish for newer clothing, and so on. Let women know they won't have to share these lists, so they can be completely honest! Play soft music while women do this.

After a few minutes, have women stop writing.

Say: *Now we're going to talk to God. As you silently reflect on each thing you've written on your list, I'd like you to ask God for contentment as it relates to that situation and then cross it off your list. Then I'd like you to go a step further and thank God for something related to that item. For example, if you're feeling bad about not being able to take a fun vacation this year, thank God for the time you've been able to spend with your neighbors because you weren't away. Find a blessing in each situation, and thank God for that.*

Play the music again as women pray silently and nurture hearts of contentment.

Forgiveness

This prayer gives women an opportunity to let go of burdensome grudges.

Prep and Supplies

- 1 brick for each woman

Tip

After this prayer, use the bricks to create a border around a flower garden at your church.

If you're meeting outside, fill paper sacks with sand instead of using bricks. Have women pour the sand out as they pray and forgive others.

Prayers

The Prayer

Stack the bricks at one end of your meeting room. Invite women to come and take a brick and hold it in outstretched arms.

Say: *As you hold the brick in outstretched arms, think of someone you need to forgive. Maybe it's your husband* (pause), *your child* (pause), *someone at work* (pause) *or even God. Hold the brick and pray, asking God to give you the strength to release the anger, resentment, hurt, or bitterness this person has brought to you.* Pause for about a minute.

Say: *Keep your eyes closed. Carefully set the brick down, and then stretch out your hands again. Spend a minute thanking God for the love and peace that he gives in exchange for our burdens.*

After about a minute, close by saying: *God, thank you for replacing our pain and anger with your love and peace. In Jesus' name, amen.*

Friendship

God places many different kinds of friends in our lives. Use this prayer to allow women to thank God for each unique friendship.

Prep and Supplies

- 1 paper cup per woman
- 1/4 cup of trail mix per woman

Place the trail mix in the cups. Note, your trail mix should include nuts, raisins, and candy such as chocolate chips.

The Prayer

Give each woman a cup with trail mix. Explain that each ingredient represents a different kind of friend in our lives.

Say: *Take out a few of the nuts from your trail mix. As you eat them, thank God for a friend who's a little nutty and makes you laugh.*

Pause for at least a minute while women do this.

Say: *Take a few pieces of the candy from your trail mix. Thank God for a friend who sweetened your life during a hard time.*

Pause for at least a minute while women do this.

Say: *Take a few of the raisins from your trail mix. Thank God for an older—and wiser—friend who's taught you something.*

Play reflective music and allow women to pray for specific friends as they eat each ingredient.

Gentleness

This prayer let's women express a gentle touch with a friend.

Prayers

Prep and Supplies

- a quality brand of lotion

Place the lotion bottles around the room, or divide it into smaller portions in small cups or nice bowls around your room. You'll want to make it easy for women to get more lotion without disrupting their prayer time.

Tip

Small sample-sized bottles of lotion would be ideal so each pair could have one.

The Prayer

Have women form pairs. Explain that you'll be praying for each other, and expressing a touch of gentleness at the same time.

Let women put lotion on their hands. Then tell women that you'd like them to take turns praying for each other. The first woman will gently massage the hands of her partner as she prays for her, and after several minutes they'll switch so the other woman is massaging and praying.

You can suggest women pray specifically for God to help them be more gentle or to grow this quality in them, or you can simply open up the time for them to pray about whatever is on their hearts while they express gentleness through the hand massage.

God's Plan/God's Will

God's plan for our lives can be hard to discern. With this prayer, women can pray for each other, asking God to guide them in all areas of life.

Prep and Supplies

You won't need any extra supplies for this prayer, although each woman will need her purse.

The Prayer

Form groups of three. Ask each woman to take three items out of her purse—the more unique each item is the better. Have trios discuss this question:

• *What part of your life does each item represent?*

For example, a movie stub might represent choices we make in what we watch or experience. A container of pain reliever could represent health. A child's school photo might represent family. (Remember, there are no right or wrong answers!) After trio members have shared, have women pass their three items to the right. Then allow trios to spend time praying for each other. As a woman holds each item, she'll pray for the owner and for God's guidance in the area of life that person talked about. Encourage women to pray for God's guidance in *all* areas of their lives.

Goodness

Use this prayer as a catalyst for celebrating God's great goodness in all areas of life!

Prep and Supplies

Photocopy the box on this page, making one copy for each woman.

The Prayer

Have women pair up and go for a walk together outside. Give each woman a copy of these instructions to use.

Prayers

- *To start, just walk around and thank God for the beauty you see outside…for the way his goodness toward his people is revealed through nature.*

- *Then spend time thanking God for the goodness he's shown you through your family.*

- *Now thank God for your friends and the way God has revealed his goodness through each of those relationships.*

- *Then thank God for your purpose in life—your job, your passions—thank God for giving you purpose and creating you to uniquely fulfill that purpose.*

- *Finally, conclude by thanking God his ultimate goodness—the sacrifice of his own Son.*

Grace

God's grace is a bit like chocolate—it's sweet, extravagant, and the perfect gift. This prayer uses chocolate to help women reflect on God's grace in their lives.

Prep and Supplies

- a bite-sized chocolate such as a small truffle or chocolate kiss for each woman. Don't skimp on quality!

- CD player and a CD with a reflective song that focuses on God's grace, such as "Amazing Grace," "Grace Flows Down," or "Your Love Is Extravagant."

Tip

This prayer works well with Psalm 34:8.

Looking for grace-focused music? Try *The Music of Chocolate Boutique* (www.group.com), which is packed with songs about God's grace.

The Prayer

Give each person a small piece of chocolate. Explain that you're going to play a song on the CD and that you'd like women to listen to the words and reflect on God's extravagant grace as the chocolate melts in their mouths. The chocolate will melt before the song is over, so women can continue to listen and reflect as the song continues.

Turn on the music, and let women close their eyes and listen as the chocolate melts in their mouths. When the song is over, quietly explain that you're going to play the song again. This time, women should silently talk to God about what his grace means to them. This will be a time of personal prayer, where women can thank God for his grace, ask for more grace, or ask to become women who pour God's grace on others.

Play the song again while women pray silently.

Prayers

Hope

In a world of disappointment, it's a comfort to know that when we put our hope in the Lord, he will not fail us. This prayer reflects that truth.

The Prayer

Say: *We're going to reflect on what the Bible says about hope, and pray back to God what's been written. Then we'll silently write out our own prayers of response to these verses. As you finish doing this with one verse, exchange your page with someone else who has a different verse. We'll continue reflecting on what God's Word says about hope and writing our prayers for about five minutes. You can use one verse, or you might do several as you have time.*

Play quiet music as women do this. After five minutes, have women keep the page they're using. They can take it home as a reminder of their own prayer for hope and the prayers of others who might have used the same verse.

Prep and Supplies

- paper
- pens

Before women arrive, type or write the text of the following verses at the top of different sheets of paper. You'll need one for each woman, and it's OK to have more than one of each verse.

2 Thessalonians 2:16-17

1 Timothy 6:17

Romans 15:13

Psalm 147:11

Psalm 42:5

Prayers

Integrity

It's easy to look around the news and see the signs of people living without integrity. Use this prayer to help women seek God's strength as they desire to live with integrity.

Prep and Supplies

- a well-sewn blanket—a homemade afghan or quilt would work best. If you have a large group, you may want to provide several blankets.

Tip

This prayer works well with Psalm 25:21.

The Prayer

Have all the women gather around the blanket. Encourage each woman to grab hold of the blanket and begin pulling. As women pull, pray aloud the following prayer, and then allow women time to finish the prayer silently:

Dear God,

This blanket is strong and well sown. Its integrity is clear to us as we pull it and it remains firm and intact. Oh, God, the temptations of this life pull at us from all sides, but we know you have called us to a firm life of integrity…a life devoted to you and your righteousness. We know we will fail and your grace will catch us, but even so we pray for your strength as we face difficult choices and daily temptations. We pray for your strength to remain pure. We pray for your strength to maintain our integrity. We want to stay firm and intact, like this blanket, even as the world tries to pull us apart. Lord, we especially pray for our integrity in these areas, we are challenged here and we know it, but our hope is in you and we pray for your strength.

Encourage women to pray silently for specific areas where their integrity has been challenged recently. After a few minutes, close the prayer with the following:

Lord, thank you for your strength. Thank you for your love. We lift these things to you and pray in Jesus' name, amen.

Joy

This prayer focuses on praising God with an attitude of joy!

Prep and Supplies

NO PREP

The Prayer

Say: *Let's have a time of prayer that will focus on praising God for his awesome attributes. Let's express the joy we have because of who God is.*

Have women think of words or very short phrases that express joy or praise for God, such as *You are mighty!* or *You are great!* Then have women randomly stand up, say their word or phrase loudly, and then sit down. Create an atmosphere of joyful praise as you call out words to God, with women quickly popping up and down all around the room!

Prayers

Kindness

This guided prayer helps women focus on kindness as it relates to many areas of their lives.

Prep and Supplies

NO PREP

The Prayer

Explain to women that you're going to lead them through a time of guided prayer. You'll read a prompt that will guide them, and they'll silently pray as directed. Allow at least one minute between these prompts:

- *God, thank you for showing your kindness to me through…*

- *Lord, reveal to me someone I can be kind to this week.*

- *Father, help me be kind to this person who I have not been getting along with recently...*

- *God, I want to grow in kindness. Show me an area where I can be more kind.*

Amen.

Prayers

Loneliness

In this prayer time, women will connect with each other in a guided prayer and musical reflection.

The Prayer

Have women form groups of three to five, and sit with those groups in circles.

Say: *I'm going to play a song that will remind us of God's presence. I'd like you to close your eyes and listen. Then, when the song is over, I'll guide your group in prayer by prompting you with specific things to pray for.*

Play the song as women silently listen and reflect. Then read these prayer prompts aloud and have groups pray aloud together. Allow at least two minutes between each prompt to let women have time for praying.

- *Pray for someone who has recently moved to a new city.*

- *Pray for someone starting a new school or job, who might not know anyone there.*

- *Pray for someone who has recently lost a loved one.*

- *Thank God for the friends you have that reach out to you when you're feeling lonely.*

Prep and Supplies

- CD player

- CD with a song related to God's presence such as "Jesus Will Still Be There," "A Mighty Fortress is Our God," "Blessed Assurance," or "You are My All in All"

Love

This prayer allows women to reflect on God's never-ending love for them.

Tip

This prayer uses Jeremiah 31:3.

The Prayer

Give each woman a daisy.

Say: *In Jeremiah 31:3, God says, "I have loved you with an everlasting love; I have drawn you with loving-kindness." Let's reflect on God's love for us by using these daisies.*

Most of us remember using a daisy to "find out" if a boy liked us or not. We'd pull off the petals and say, "He loves me. He loves me not." Then, when we pulled off the last petal, we thought we knew whether we were loved or not. But Jeremiah 31:3 tells us that God always *loves us. He doesn't randomly change his mind.*

I'm going to play some music softly in the background. While you listen, pull petals off your daisy until they're all gone. As you pull off each petal, softly say, "He loves me," or "Lord, you love me," aloud. Let this time be a reflective moment between you and God as you consider his boundless love for you, and thank him for that.

Play music softly while women quietly pray and reflect.

Prayers

Obedience

This prayer allows for quiet reflection and meditation in the area of growing in obedience.

Prayers

Prep and Supplies

None are required, but playing soft music in the background is nice.

The Prayer

Say: *As I read some questions aloud, think about how they relate to you, and talk to God about these.* Allow at least two minutes between each comment to allow for reflection and prayer.

- *Some parents say, "I'm going to count to three" to give their children time to think about obeying instead of requiring immediate obedience. Where is God allowing you time to think about obedience? Talk to God about those areas of your life.*

- *We wouldn't count to three and wait for obedience if a child was stepping in front of a speeding car. There are times when immediate obedience is essential. Where is God asking you to be immediately obedient? Talk to God about those areas of your life.*

- *What are the areas of your life where you have been disobedient? Ask God for forgiveness for those areas now.*

You may want to have women join with another person and share about what they learned during this time of reflection and prayer. Encourage them to pray for each other in the area of obedience in the coming week or month.

Patience

It's tough for women to patiently wait on God's timing. This sweet, reflective prayer gives women time to ask God for patience.

The Prayer

Give each woman a hard candy. Direct women to hold the candy while they think of an area of life in which it's hard to be patient. Women might reflect on their children, trouble at work, or waiting for God to send a special friend. Then read aloud Psalm 46:10: *"Be still, and know that I am God!"*

Say: *Put your candy in your mouth and enjoy the sweetness of waiting on God's timing. Spend a few minutes in prayer. As you pray, imagine the candy is that issue in life. Imagine God working away at it in a unique way—like only God can. You'll finish your prayer when you finish your candy.*

Play reflective music while women spend time praying. It's OK if this prayer time takes five minutes or a little longer. What may seem like a long time of "silence," can actually be a powerful time for God to speak!

Prep and Supplies

- 1 piece of hard candy per woman

Tip

This prayer uses Psalm 46:10.

Prayers

Peace

Peace isn't a sappy feeling of contentment... it's when God stills the storms of anxiety inside us as we rely on him. Use this prayer to help women ask God to give them peace in life's storms.

The Prayer

Form trios and give each trio a jar you prepared ahead of time.

Say: *In the Bible, Jesus calmed storms, turning raging seas into smooth and calm—peaceful—waters.*

Direct women to pass their jar around their trio for one minute. As women pass the jar, they should shake it and say a word or phrase about something that robs them of peace. Women might say, "News," "unemployment," "sickness," or "gossip." After one minute, ask trios to set their "storm" in the middle of their circle, join hands, and pray for the things they mentioned. When women finish praying, they can look and see that the "storm" has calmed.

Prep and Supplies

- 1 small jar with a lid per three women

- vegetable oil

- water

Fill the jars about halfway with water, and then add a few tablespoons of oil. Screw the lids on tightly.

Tip

If you've got an adventurous group of women, gather as a large group outside around a child's pool filled with water. Women can lift the pool slightly to make waves...and they might actually get a little wet!

Pride

Pride is an issue of reflection—how we see ourselves and how we hope others see us. This prayer will give women a reminder that will help them give arrogance and pride to God...daily!

Prep and Supplies

- pens
- 1 large index card (at least 4x6 inches) per woman
- CD player and CD of reflective music

The Prayer

Give each woman an index card and a pen. Direct women to close their eyes and silently reflect on areas of pride in their lives. You might want to play a song like "Turn Your Eyes Upon Jesus" during this time.

Say: *Many times, pride is an issue of looks. How we see ourselves and how we hope others see us. Spend five minutes writing out a simple prayer, asking God to humble your heart. You'll tape this prayer at eye-level, on the mirror you use most often.*

Play reflective music while women write out their prayers.

Tip

You may want to take this one step further and have women make a smaller prayer card to fit over a purse-sized mirror (or a compact mirror). When women open their compact, they'll be reminded to give areas of pride to God.

Purity

Prayers

Many women deal with a heavy sense of shame for things they have done and things that have been done to them. While you may not be able to lead the women in your group through complete psychological healing through this prayer, you can help them understand that purity is a gift they can receive by simply praying.

Prep and Supplies

- 1 blank sheet of paper per woman
- pens or pencils
- stacks of sticky notes
- CD player and CD reflective music

Tip

This prayer uses Hebrews 9:14.

During this prayer, choose meaningful songs about Jesus' sacrifice for our sins such as "Only the Blood of Jesus," "Amazing Grace," "O How He Loves You and Me," or "The Old Rugged Cross."

The Prayer

Give each woman a paper, pen, and a stack of sticky notes. Explain that when God created us, he intended for us to be pure, holy, and beautiful. We were spotless—like the blank paper in front of each person. Discuss how sin has stained our hearts, minds, and souls. Remind women that stain has come in two forms: things we have done, and things done to us.

Have women write separate examples of sin that has stained their lives on separate sticky notes. Direct women to stick the notes to their sheets of paper.

Read Hebrews 9:14. Encourage women to tell God that they're sorry for the things on the notes that they've done and to ask God to make them clean from the things on the notes that have been done to them. As they pray for each item, have women pull off the corresponding sticky note and crumple it up. After the prayer, remind women that it really is that simple. Through Jesus, they really are completely pure again—whether they feel like it or not.

Purpose

What is God's purpose for your life? Once you discover it, what will you do? This prayer will encourage women to take steps toward living the life God intended for them.

The Prayer

Have women write down one thing they believe is a part of God's purpose for them on the slip of paper. Remind women that "God's purpose" doesn't have to be a grand or "deep" mission. It might be as simple as "love others" or "show God's mercy to my family."

Direct women to set their paper on the ground somewhere that's away from others. Then have women stand about five feet from their papers.

Say: *God wants you to take steps everyday toward living out his purpose for your life. Take one step toward your paper, then stop and pray, asking God to help you in one specific way. Then take another step, stop, and pray. Continue taking steps and praying, until you've reached the slip of paper.*

Allow a few moments for women to pray and take steps toward God's purpose for their lives.

Prep and Supplies

- 1 slip of paper per woman

- pens or pencils

Tip

This is a great prayer to do outside. If weather or space doesn't allow you to go outside, plan to do this active prayer in a large, open room.

Prayers

Self-Control

Some things really "push our buttons." Use this prayer to allow women to share some of their "hot buttons," and then to pray for each other.

Prep and Supplies

- 1 remote control for every four women. Women won't actually *use* the remote controls, so don't worry about batteries.

The Prayer

Form groups of four and give each group a remote control. Talk about how you push different buttons on the remote to bring about a certain action. Have women pass the remote around their group and share a few things that "push their buttons" and cause them to lose control. Women might share "when my kids talk back I lose my temper" or "when I'm at parties it's hard for me not to overeat."

When everyone has shared, have women set the remote in the center of their group. Have them join hands with the members of their group and pray for each other in specific ways. Direct women to ask God to be in control of their lives.

Service

This prayer puts service into action! You'll take women outside and pray as you walk.

The Prayer

Have women form pairs or trios. Explain that you're going to leave the building and walk around the neighborhood. As women walk past homes, schools, or businesses, they should pray aloud with their partners for the people who live, study, or work there.

This time of prayer will be a true act of service to your community, asking for God's love to be made known in your community, and for people to come to know Jesus personally.

Encourage groups to spread out in the neighborhood—some might even want to drive to different locations to cover more area. Tell women how long they should walk (such as for half an hour) and pray. It can be exciting to have groups return to your starting location and share what happened on their prayer walk. Did they meet someone? Share about Jesus with someone? Have any special insights as they were walking and praying?

Prayers

Sharing Your Faith

Even though it can be scary to share our faith, it can also be life-saving for someone else. This prayer will help women identify people to whom they can offer the life-saving message of Jesus' love.

Prep and Supplies

- 1 roll of assorted LifeSavers candies for each woman

- CD player and CD of reflective music

If you can't find the candy in rolls, you may be able to find individually-wrapped rolled candy in the aisle with the bagged candies. Just have each woman take a handful of the candies from a bowl.

The Prayer

Say: *In John 6:68, Simon Peter asked Jesus this question: "Lord, to whom would we go? You have the words that give eternal life." We're going to use this verse in our prayer today.*

Form pairs and give each person a roll of LifeSavers candies. Direct partners to say aloud the question from John 6:68, substituting the opposite partner's name for the word "you." For example, "Amber has the words that give eternal life."

Say: *You have something that can give eternal life to your spouse, a friend, a co-worker, or your children. You can be a life-saver! Open your roll of candy and look at the first color in the roll.* (Pause while women do this.) *Think of someone who doesn't know about Jesus. Maybe you have a green candy and it reminds you of your friend who's really into gardening…she's got a green thumb! Take out the candy and pop it in your mouth, then tell your partner about that person. Pray for each other, asking God to give you the right words—words that give eternal life to that person.*

Play reflective music while women pray for each other.

Tip

This prayer uses John 6:68.

Tip

Encourage women to use the LifeSavers as a prayer prompt. Each time women pull out the candies, they can pray for someone who doesn't know Christ.

Spiritual Growth

As we pray, fellowship, and listen to God, our faith grows stronger. Use this prayer to help women explore ways they can strengthen their faith.

Prep and Supplies

- Bibles
- pens or pencils
- 8½ x 11-inch sheets of paper

Tip

This prayer uses Galatians 5:22-23.

The Prayer

Ask women to look up Galatians 5:22-23 and write out the passage on a sheet of paper.

Say: *As we grow in our faith, these are things we'll see in our lives. Things like love, joy, peace, and patience deepen and strengthen our faith.*

Direct each woman to fold her paper in half (top to bottom), and silently pray for one of the fruit of the Holy Spirit to be evident in her life. After a minute, direct women to turn the paper around so the thinner side is at the top, and again fold the paper in half (top to bottom), praying for a different fruit of the Spirit. Continue until women have folded their papers up to six times.

Say: *It's nearly impossible to fold a sheet of paper more than six times. Each time you fold the paper, it doubles in thickness. What a cool way to view spiritual growth. We truly do want our friendship with God to grow…exponentially!*

Then close by praying: *Loving God, strengthen our faith. As we grow closer to you, help us to show love, peace, patience, kindness, goodness, gentleness, and self-control. In Jesus' name, amen.*

Prayers

Temptation

We're bombarded with temptation every day. This active prayer gets women thinking about all the ways they're tempted, and let's them put those before God.

Prep and Supplies

- paper
- pens or pencils
- large wastebasket

Tip

This prayer uses Matthew 26:41.

The Prayer

Give women paper and pens. **Say:** *On each sheet of paper, write a word to represent things that tempt you. Don't put your name on these. As you write each one, crumple that into a ball and set it beside you until you have a pile of paper balls.*

When each woman has several paper balls, have them gather their supply, and start throwing them at each other. Really! When women run out of paper balls they can collect others from the floor and toss those, too! Let this wildness go on for at least a minute—some women might even gather a few others and get a team competition going!

Then have everyone sit down.

Say: *Do you ever feel bombarded with temptations? Like there are so many hitting you and coming at you right and left—like they were just now? Matthew 26:41 says, "Keep watch and pray, so that you will not give in to temptation. For the spirit is willing, but the body is weak!"*

Let's avoid giving in to these temptations that bombard us by doing just what this verse says. Pray!

Have women gather the balls of paper and put them all into one large wastebasket, and then gather around this and pray together against all the temptations that are represented there. Let women pray for each other to be strong against temptations, and ask God to help them continue to pray each day for God's strength.

Trust

This prayer allows women to trust others as a symbol of trusting God.

Prep and Supplies

NO PREP

The Prayer

Have each woman find a partner. Ask women to stand back to back with their shoulders touching.

Say: *With your shoulders still touching, take one step away from each other.* Pause for women to do this, and then say: *Keep taking small steps away from each other as you lean against the shoulders of your partner. See how far you can go, trusting the other person to hold you up as you hold her up!*

This may get noisy with laughter as women see how far they can step while trusting each other. Once women have settled on the distance of how far they can step while still trusting, have them pray for each other while in this position. Encourage them to ask God for the ability to trust him more, just as they are trusting their partners to keep them from falling right now.

Then let women step back toward each other and end with a hug!

Prayers

Unity/Community/ Body of Christ

Women will create a circle of paper dolls to represent members of Christ's body in the world or in their community.

Prep and Supplies

- pencils

- crayons or colored pencils

- scissors

- photocopies of page 105

- extra-large sheets of wrapping paper, pre-cut into squares. You can also use your local newspaper!

Make one of the paper dolls circle ahead of time to show as a sample.

Tip

Remember, for the dolls to connect, the figure's hands must touch the folded edge of the triangle. Don't cut the hands!

The Prayer

Show women the paper doll circle that you've made ahead of time, and explain that each woman will make one of these as a prayer reminder. Make the supplies and copies of the folding and cutting instructions available, and let each woman make her own paper doll circle.

When women unfold their circles of dolls they'll see eight figures. Ask them to write the names of different Christian churches from your community on these, one church per figure. Or have them write one missionary your church supports on each figure. If time permits, women can use crayons or colored pencils to decorate each figure and give them personality!

When all are completed, have women stand, as the dolls do, in a circle with hands held. Pray together for those who are represented on the paper doll figures, that there would be unity of heart and purpose among these people. Encourage women to take these figures home and hang them in the laundry room, kitchen, or other place they'll be seen as a reminder to pray throughout the week.

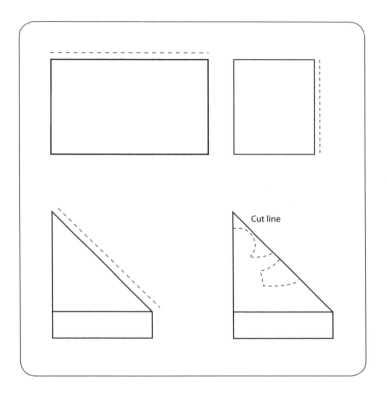

Cut line

Warm-Ups, Wrap-Ups, and Prayers for Women's Groups

Wisdom

Solomon compared wisdom to a light that guides our path. This prayer will allow women time to pray for God's wisdom.

Prep and Supplies

- 1 votive candle in a small holder per woman
- matches or lighters
- CD player and CD with soft music

Tip

If you're uncomfortable using candles, you can give each woman a small flashlight.

This prayer uses Ecclesiastes 2:13-14.

The Prayer

Say: *Ecclesiastes 2:13-14 says, "Wisdom is better than foolishness, just as light is better than darkness. For the wise can see where they are going, but fools walk in the dark."*

Give each woman a candle and a book of matches, then direct women to scatter around the room. Dim the lights and play reflective music. Allow women to spend time in this darkened room, praying for God's wisdom in their lives.

After a couple of minutes, light a candle and read the passage aloud again. Direct women to light their own candles. Ask women to pray again, asking God to light their paths and to show them ways to walk in his wisdom. After a minute, direct women to slowly bring their candles to the middle of the room and set them on a table.

Join in a circle around the candles and close in prayer.

Worry

This prayer idea is also a visual reminder of God's faithful provision in our lives.

Prep and Supplies

- 1-foot length or longer of grosgrain ribbon for each woman. Try to find a cute striped or polka-dot design, or a variety of colors.

Tip

This prayer uses Matthew 6:25-34.

The Prayer

Give each woman one of the ribbons—or let them choose the one they like best. Ask women to use this ribbon to add a bit of beauty to what they're wearing. Some may wish to wear it in their hair or around their necks, while others might use is as a watchband or shoelace. Feel free to get a little silly!

Read Matthew 6:25-34 aloud.

Say: *Let's let this little bit of colorful "clothing" that we've added to our attire today be a reminder of God's faithful provision in the lives of the ones he loves. When we feel worried about food, clothing—or anything—we can be confident that God knows our needs and cares.*

Take time for women to pray either in small groups or with partners, expressing specific worries that they need to turn over to God, and asking him for peace as they release those to him. Let women take the ribbons home and tie them on a purse or car rear-view mirror as a reminder of God's faithfulness as we offer our worries to him.

Scripture Index

Discover

CRAFTS GALORE:

THE ULTIMATE GUIDE FOR GIRLFRIENDS!

Over 40 quality crafts you'll want to try! Let *Crafts Galore!* act like glue and bring good friends and new neighbors together. Each craft is easy to make, easy on the pocketbook, and a fun delight for the eyes. Women will want to keep these crafts—and they'll love sharing them with others.

ISBN 978-0-7644-3657-4
www.group.com/women